SPANISH DANCING

Spanish Dancing

A handbook on steps, style, castanets and dancing.

By

Helen Wingrave and Robert Harrold

Foreword by Frank and Peggy Spencer

Published by Planned Action Limited

ISBN 0 85936 000 8

A tape recording (3¾ speed) of the music in this handbook is obtainable for use in class teaching or competitive work. **Price 75p (including postage)**

From Miss Barbara Lander, 82 Kempshott Road, Streatham, London SW16.

A record (7" EP) of guitar music which has been recorded in Spain is obtainable from Planned Action Limited. 12 Dene Way, Speldhurst, Tunbridge Wells, Kent.

This record has musical sections for the exercises on castanets, arms and foot beats as well as for the dances described in this book.

Published by Planned Action Ltd
12 Dene Way, Speldhurst, Tunbridge Wells, Kent.
Printed by Photo Precision Limited, St. Ives, Huntingdon
Produced by PJH Graphic Services.
Cover illustration by Brian Shaw.

CONTENTS

ACKNOWLEDGEMENTS

Helen Wingrave and Robert Harrold are greatly indebted to the many dancers and teachers in several countries who have so generously given them instruction and help in the art of Spanish dancing.

In the course of many years studying in London and Spain, both authors have come to appreciate a subject that is vast, never-ending and very little documented. Teachers and schools of Spanish dancing vary in their approach; there are changes in technical terms and names of steps. Increasing popularity has altered the whole aspect of the dancing over recent years and there are differing opinions as to what is right and wrong. But while dances come and go and costume styles change, the basic requirements remain the same.

Many sources have contributed to the compilation of this book, but grateful thanks are particularly extended to Elsa Brunelleschi of London, the Pericet family both in Madrid and Seville, *El Cojo* and Adelita Domingo in Seville, Trini Borull, the famous teacher and dancer now living in the Gran Canaria, and Juan Garcia.

Credit for first suggesting that a book on these lines would be of great help to the dancer studying Paso Doble must go to Peggy Spencer, the well-known teacher of Ballroom and Latin-American dancing who, as an active committee member of the Latin American Branch of the Imperial Society, introduced a lecture on the Spanish approach to the Paso Doble presented at the Imperial Congress in 1971.

The authors express their thanks to Frank and Peggy Spencer for writing a foreword and also to the Imperial Society of Teachers of Dancing who have, through their National and Latin American Branches, given them the opportunity to pass on their knowledge to other teachers. Appreciations for their contributions are also extended to Peter Herridge who produced the illustrations and Sylvia Forde for the help given by the Spanish Tourist Office, and Sr. Luis Villalba, Minister for Cultural Affairs, Spanish Embassy.

Finally, our thanks to the many musicians who have helped collect and interpret the music, especially to Barbara Lander for editing it for the piano and Francis Eling for copying,.

FOREWORD

Dancing in all its forms is a most enjoyable kind of recreation. In recent years, Latin music and dancing has emerged as a vital part of all programmes, but surely one of the most intriguing rhythms and forms of dance is the Paso Doble and Spanish flamenco style. The stirring music, exciting dance steps, foot beating, elegant poise and castanet playing have gained still greater popularity as the highlight of holidaymaking in Spain and South America.

This book which Helen Wingrave and Robert Harrold have written and compiled is designed to help all who would like to study this type of dancing and music in some detail. The use of hands, body and feet which are such important features of the dance have been dealt with in a way that can be understood and practised even by an elementary dancer, as are the essential exercises which the authors recommend.

Much more than this, however, the book will appeal to those who may not want to 'have a go' themselves but who can gain from it a keener appreciation in watching the dances and listening to the exciting music. The intending visitor to Spain can enjoy his holiday all the more for having a prior knowledge, and the returning tourist can re-live the enjoyment of a night club session by learning to play the castanets bought as a souvenir.

Paso Doble was originally a dance simply depicting the actions of the Matador during a bull fight when, of course, he would not release hold of his cape; the dancer would thus not release hold of his lady. It has now progressed from that style and many flamenco and Spanish movements have been introduced into the ballroom version of the dance. Knowledge of this branch of dancing is lacking, and this book will be of tremendous value to teachers, coaches and competitors in their efforts to attain the authentic 'look' to the lines, poses, heel and toe beats and hand positions used in the choreography of the Paso Doble for ballroom, cabaret and competition presentations.

This is the first book that has been able to give us real assistance in a way that can be both understood and readily applied when the basic fundamentals have been practised and grasped.

We are very grateful to Helen and Robert for the tremendous amount of research and work that has now resulted in this wonderful handbook and hope that through this medium more people will find the joy of dancing to Spanish music and experience the added exhilaration that comes to those who know how and why.

Frank and Peggy Spencer

INTRODUCTION

A magical part of the Spanish scene is the exciting music and dance, especially that of the South. As long ago as Roman times, dancers from Cadiz were in great demand as entertainers for Roman banquets. Spanish dancers are infinitely more popular today, in the many shows, cabarets and entertainments throughout Spain, and for the dance companies which tour the world. Who can resist the infectious rhythms of Spanish dance music? Even those who have not yet travelled to Spain succumb to the excitement through the medium of television.

Holidaymakers by the million return from Spain with castanets as souvenirs, flamenco-dressed dolls to adorn the home, and vivid memories of the warmth and spectacle of Spanish entertainment. Now, with the help of this book, they can live again those colourful moments, appreciate a little of the history and significance of the music and movements, and even learn to play those castanets!

The book is written for the enjoyment of all who have been thrilled by the art of Spanish dancing and especially those who would like to attempt some of the intricacies of this most exciting dance style. It also certainly aims to help the many professional and amateur dancers who study the Paso Doble in the Latin American ballroom world.

The dance forms found in Spain can be classified as:

> Regional or Peasant*
> Classical, popular in the 19th century
> Theatre or stylised arrangements
> Gypsy or Flamenco

It is not intended to present a serious study of the Spanish dance - to become an expert dancer one requires a depth of interpretation and tuition in technique. Rather this book is designed to give pleasure, to be of guidance in the basic steps and interpretation of style. The form discussed is Flamenco, the most popular style in Spain. It is essential that the basic work is well studied; the stance of the body, use of the arms and castanets, action and technique of the foot. All this should be mastered before attempting to perform one of the dances. Spanish dancers spend many hours of hard work perfecting their movements, and the reader must not expect results too quickly.

At the end of the chapter entitled *The Development of Style* is a series of exercises which combine the movements and are divided into the four sections, (A) Arms, (B) Head, (C) Hands and (D) Footwork. When practising, it is advisable to learn the (A) section in each exercise first.

When familiar with the (A) in exercises 1-7, add the (B) section, then combine (A) and (B) throughout and gradually build up the technique in this way by adding the next section.

The dances included in this handbook are not technically difficult but do require some study and thought. They have been shortened and simplified for the beginner and serve as a good introduction to correct interpretation. The three solos described are complete and can easily be performed. The Spanish dancer usually performs in a small area of a cafe, patio, cave or in cabaret, the focus being on the execution, style and quality of the dancer rather than on the choreographic design and floor pattern. The woman should have lovely arm and hand movements which contrast

*La Canastilla from Northern Spain and a Basque Fandango are given in the authors' book *Regional Dances of Europe, Vol. 1.*

with the strength and virility of her partner. The use of castanets combined with dance movement can be very exciting, though difficult to achieve, as successful castanet playing requires plenty of practise and perseverance.

Readers proficient in the Paso Doble but lacking an authentic Spanish style will find close study of the basic work invaluable, and some of the steps can easily be adapted for ballroom presentation. The various arm and body positions are worthy of special study and of incorporation in the dance routine, as the more a Latin American dancer understands the traditional form, the stronger and more convincing will be the effect on the ballroom floor.

For easier reference, an Anglicised version has been used for the names of all the steps mentioned in this book.

The Development of Style

POSTURE

The characteristic stance and balance of the body

Before attempting the steps and dances, it is essential to understand and maintain the special carriage of the body, a most important feature of the Spanish dancer. It may be easy to hold the correct position for a few minutes in a static pose but the test is to sustain it throughout a dance. Costume plays a significant part in the development of posture. The lady's dress has a very tight fitting bodice ending at hip level or, in some cases, well below the hips. The bodice is made to fit the body like a leotard or swimsuit, so any faulty posture is very evident. The tight bodice helps develop the uplift through the body, whereas a waisted or belted dress can hide the reverse action when the body sinks into the hips.

In the man's costume there is a similar development of body line. The trousers are tight fitting and start five or six inches above the waist. This encourages the stretch and lift of the upper body out of the hips, which is more difficult to achieve when trousers are belted in at waist level.

The position and carriage of the body are slightly different for the man and the lady.

The Lady
Stand with both feet together, the weight slightly forward over the balls of the feet. Pull the abdomen well in, lock the buttocks to avoid a hollow back. Lift the rib cage up and out of the waist, so elongating the spine. (Due to the amount of sitting we do in everyday life, there is a general tendency to allow the body to sink into the hips, thus producing the so-called 'spare-tyre'!). Try to imagine a band of air round the waist between ribs and hips. The chest should be held up and forward with a feeling of pride. The shoulders should be kept well down and back with the shoulder blades held firmly. With the pulling down of the shoulder blades, the neck will lengthen and a good, balanced line is given to the head. The chin is lifted slightly with the head and neck complementing the line of the dancer.

The Man
The position for the man is very similar to that for the lady. Stand with both feet together with the weight slightly over the front part of the feet. Feel a control and extension through the body. There must be strength throughout the man's posture and he must always dominate his partner and prove a foil for her. His line follows that of the lady, with the up-lift through the abdomen, locked buttocks, shoulders down, chest out but without such a strong arch in the upper spine. The man has altogether a straighter line in the back, the lady by contrast showing the curves. In some poses and bull fighting movements, there is a slight push forward

with the hips which accents the line in the upper body. The man keeps his hips well controlled with very little hip action and no exaggerated sideways swing. Many of the bull fighting passes which have been incorporated into Paso Doble routines require the man to develop a sideways bend. If the right side of the body contracts at waist level, then the left side is well stretched. (Avoid lifting the shoulders or rolling them forward on any of these movements which would give a twisted line.)

There is a misguided theory that a Spanish dancer must arch in the back at waist level. The arch or curve actually develops above the waist and continues to the neck. Pushing back the pelvis gives an ugly and exaggerated line and can cause harm. If the upper body is well held and sustained, the hips will find a correct line and the arch develop. This position of the body should never become rigid or so tense that it is difficult to move, it should be an easy and well-poised base on which to add the arm movements, poses, steps and foot beats.

A famous teacher once said, 'The upper body should always be lifted towards the ceiling and the lower body driven into the floor'. Thinking of the body in two halves will help in tackling some of the dance movements. If the body line is correct then, when dancing, there will not be the exaggerated hip movements which are so often thought of as being sexy and Spanish! The hips should move only slightly as when carrying or balancing a heavy jar on one's head. (The movement of the hips should stem from the action of the feet, not be imposed on to the body and so give an unnatural effect.)

In the Flamenco or Gypsy dances, the position of the body has a very strong arch.

The Line of the Head

The carriage and line of the head can be one of the most expressive in the body. If the neck is tense or the chin either lifted too high or tucked in, the visual aspect of a pose or movement can be spoilt. With the correct posture, the shoulders well down, upper back arched and chest out, the head should establish a well poised position, indicative of pride and dignity.

The line of the head is accentuated by the hair styles adopted by the women, the hair pulled back away from the face and caught in a bun at the nape of the neck. Artificial flowers are sometimes pinned into the side of the bun or along one side of the head, following the line of the ear. A large flower or comb is sometimes worn centre back of the head. Rather large circular earrings are also popular. These various trimmings all help to accentuate a good head line, but too much paraphern- alia on the head can, however, be fussy and very distracting.

The head should move freely, without strain, able to turn from side to side following a sharp foot action. The chin can drop slightly towards the right or left shoulder on a step where the foot is extended to the side, the vision of the eyes being directed to the foot. On turns or passes, the head is used either sharply or smoothly, according to the speed and quality of the music. When dancing with a partner, a good eye contact should be kept for the head to follow the steps or movements thus producing good line.

The man also shows a good poised line of the head but he is inclined to lower the chin and have firmer positions. Usually the male dancer is slightly taller than his partner, his eye line will be lowered when dancing with her, so giving a natural incline of the head. In Paso Doble work, during cape movements and bull fighting passages, his eyes should focus on an imaginary bull. On some passes the bull will lower his head to charge or, on other more complicated passes, the head is lowered and then will move upwards. If he follows his partner who simulates these passes, the head will show a good line. To be over-tense or strained shows in the neck and the whole effect becomes rather stiff and wooden. Many dancers, particularly if they have studied only ballroom techniques when tackling Paso Doble or Latin dancing, find difficulty in using the head. A tendency to move the head and the body in one piece can give a very faulty overall picture and line.

In Flamenco dances the head is used with more abandon and freedom, the posture a little more exaggerated than in the Andalusian style. The gypsy girl will sometimes favour loose hair, perhaps just pulled back and caught with a flower. Head movements are quick and sharp with a great deal of head and hair tossing. Care is needed not to exaggerate these movements of the head – a Spanish gypsy can possibly succeed but bad imitations can look farcical!

ARMS

Basic arm positions and movements

Unlike ballet, there are no set arm positions in Spanish dancing but the arms do move through certain basic designs. Once the control of the body is mastered, use of the arms is the next development. The arms play an important part in the dance; they either complement a pose, or a pose can be taken and the arms will move through various positions. When studying arm movements, keep a fluid action to blend with the line of the body or dance movement. Tension in arm practice produces angular lines; the designs are curved and based on the letter 'S' rather than a 'Z'. The arms should not become wrapped round the body; there must always be a feeling of space and air when the arms move from one position to another. It is very seldom that a straight and stretched arm line is used; however, it does occur in some bull fighting passes and movements in the Paso Doble. When lifting the arms above the head, the shoulders should remain in place, the arms whether being raised or passing through the various positions, should move easily within the shoulder socket. With the correct posture and feeling of uplift in the chest, the arms develop the Spanish line and style.

Before practising some of the set exercises, a study of the various positions is required.

Position 1

a   The arms are down each side of the body, elbows slightly bent and the palms turned in towards the hips.

b   Crossed. Both arms are behind the body with the wrists either touching or close together, the palms facing outwards and the hands stretched downwards. The elbows are slightly bent and the arms held away from the body.

Position 2

Both arms are out to the side of the body and carried slightly forward, with curved elbow and with the palms facing down. (In some bull fighting and Paso Doble movements, when simulating the action of the cape, one arm can have a more stretched line with the palm facing forward.)

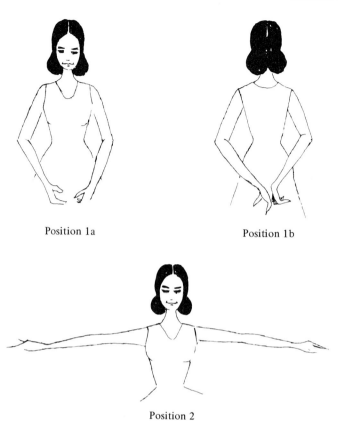

Position 1a   Position 1b

Position 2

Position 3

One arm is curved overhead, the hand with the palm down and over the crown of the head. The other arm is relaxed in 2nd position.

Position 3

Position 4

a One arm is curved overhead as in 3rd position, the other is curved in front of the body in line with the chest. The palm can either be facing inwards to the body or turned parallel to the floor. There should be a continuous flowing line between the two arms.

b Crossed. One arm is curved forward as in 4th position, the other behind the back as in the 1st position (b) crossed. There should be a continuous flowing line from the forward hand through the arms to the other hand lowered at the back.

c Crossed. One arm is curved forward as in 4th position, the other arm is bent. The man - the palm of the hand on the hip with the fingers forward; the girl - holding her skirt against the hip.

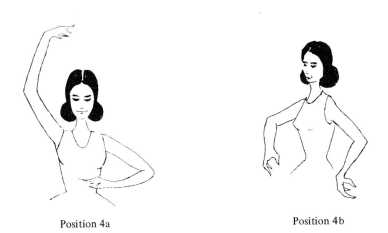

Position 4a   Position 4b

Position 4c

Position 5

Both arms are curved overhead, the hands with the palms down are well over the crown of the head. This position can also be taken with the wrists crossed and the palms down, or with the back of the wrists together and the palms facing out.

Position 5

The Gateway

Both arms are curved forward at chest level.

The Gateway

When performing one of the dances included in this book or a Paso Doble sequence, the exact position of the arms need not be rigidly followed, a certain flexibility is allowed for individual interpretation. The positions given are only a guide; a dancer, according to the mood, will perhaps lift the arm a little higher or lower it slightly, but keeping the movement and design within the basic positions.

HANDS

Basic hand positions and movements

Once the arm positions are established and the set exercises practised, a little more detail can be applied to the various hand movements.

In Spanish dancing, the hands, when not playing the castanets, have two main actions, to produce a firm or a relaxed movement or position. The fingers are extended, separated or grouped with either an expression of strength or held in the one position but with a relaxed feeling (Fig.1). The position of the arm and quality of

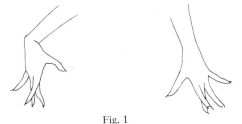

Fig. 1

the movement depends on the style of music or dance technique. If a very sharp, quick turn has been executed, ending in an arrested pose, then the strength of that movement will be shown right through to the ends of the fingers. A sudden pose can be held firmly for a moment, then could be followed by arm and hand movements of a relaxed quality; moving through various positions.

Hand Positions

The hand is often held with what is known as a broken wrist line. If the arms are

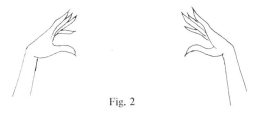

Fig. 2

placed in 5th position, the line of the hands is broken from the wrist with palms facing down over the head (Fig.2). This broken line is also found in the 3rd and 4th positions where one arm is raised overhead. When the arms are in 2nd position or one arm is out at the side as in 3rd position, the wrist does not break so dramatically. A feeling of strength or relaxation is still evident but the hand continues the line of the arm.

A Stretched Hand

The hand is nearly always held with the fingers separated, although an exception is found in the Paso Doble when the man uses a flat hand with the fingers together, characteristic when performing bull fighting passes. Ladies usually have hand positions as shown in Fig.1. The men follow the same line but with less exaggeration.

A Relaxed Hand

The quieter moments in a dance are often shown with relaxed hand movements, especially those performed by the lady. A relaxed hand follows the same pattern and grouping as the stretched position, but without the tension and force. The body retains the carriage but arms and hands move with a more fluid quality. The arm exercises should be practised with both strength and a relaxed approach.

Hand Rotations

Often during a solo or duet the dancer will strike a pose, then follow with various rotary actions of the hands which can be very beautiful and reminiscent of the Indian and Arab legacies found in the Flamenco and Andalusian styles.

When performing rotations, the hand and fingers are generally relaxed and the turning action of the hand is made only at the wrist.

Hands rotate through Figs. 2, 3 and 4, returning to original position at Fig.2.

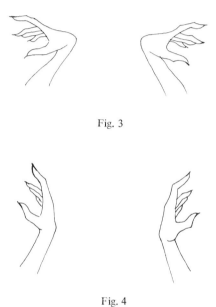

Fig. 3

Fig. 4

When these hand movements are performed by a man, they are much stronger with the fingers held together and a flatter hand. The wrist action is the same but the hand lacks the flexibility and softness of the lady's.

Finger Snapping

Some Spanish dancers can snap their fingers together with a sound that rings out like a pistol shot, achieved by having fairly strong fingers and finding the knack of using them. The middle or second finger presses on the tip of the thumb pad, the finger then slides sharply down to hit the palm with a sharp crack. There is no rule of how this snap is achieved; but one Spanish teacher advised placing the ring or third finger on the cushion of the thumb as it was the action of the middle finger snapping against it and the thumb pad which made the sound.

The fingers should not snap throughout a whole dance with a monotonous regularity, but to accent a passage of steps, or a particular step or beat. Snapping is also used to emphasise a pose, or as the arms pass into various positions. A pose may be taken in a 3rd or 4th arm position and the fingers clicked as the arm is moved into a 5th position. Whenever used, the snapping should always be rhythmical.

Hand Clapping

The clapping action is very much a part of the Flamenco scene. Dancers sit in the traditional half circle waiting for their turn to dance, giving support to fellow artists with lively hand clapping and encouraging calls. Hand claps can also be executed by a dancer during the solo.

When clapping, the hands are usually held at chest level, either to the right or left side of the chest, or raised level with the shoulders or even taken a little higher, above the shoulder at head level. The elbows are lifted slightly when clapping in any of these positions to give a good line and make the movement easier to perform. The right hand is at right angles to the left hand, (not held together as in a prayer position). The hands can make two sounds: (i) a dry, crisp clap or (ii) a deeper more muted tone.

To produce (i), the first three fingers of the right hand strike sharply against the flat palm of the firm left hand. (ii) the hands are curved and cupped slightly. The right hand still beats on the left, but the cupped palms together give a hollow sound. The tone of the clap is varied according to the mood, rhythm and type of dance. A dancer may perform a syncopated clap, stamping his feet on the beat and clapping on the 'and' or 'off' beat. In the introduction to the dance Soleares there is an example of claps performed on various unaccented beats of the musical phrase.

The clapping sound can be used very effectively in couple dances or with the Paso Doble. The dancers can clap in a syncopated rhythm whilst executing a step, either side by side, facing each other or one facing forward and one in the opposite direction, with right shoulders together, looking at each other over the right shoulders and clapping to the left side. It could also be performed by the man in a held pose while his partner performed a step in front of him. In dance choreography there are numerous ways to use claps but too many can become noisy and lose impact.

LEGS

The use of relaxation and tension in the knees

Having discussed the upper body, the posture, head, arms and hands, we come to the use of the legs and feet. A certain rhythm has been developed in the upper limbs and they are moved with a controlled action, this feeling is passed through to the legs. Part of good posture includes a firm pelvic girdle; when this is maintained, the action of the legs will develop more through the thighs and knees and not from the hips. A slight movement in the hips is necessary, but too much freedom and swaying in the hips is wrong. The lady has a little more freedom than a man, but should avoid any exaggeration, allow the thighs and feet to do the work then the action of the hips will then develop naturally.

The legs have two main actions: (i) relaxed knees which give the movement a feeling of emphasis into the ground; (ii) pulled up, stretched knees and thighs, to give a feeling of confidence and strength. Action (i) is used for all foot beats and when performing the various steps. The knees should be slightly relaxed and come just over the toes when executing beats. Action (ii) the stretched leg - is found in the various held positions, bull fighting passes and some Paso Doble movements. When standing on a straight leg there is a feeling of contact with the ground, the upper body maintaining its poised line. A typical pose is for one leg to be straight and the other relaxed, the weight poised forward and taken on the straight supporting leg without a sideways drop of the hips.

Spanish dances, other than Regional and classical, are usually performed in a fairly small dancing area which means that large leg actions should be avoided. When dancing with a partner the steps are small and neat. Any lunges or kneels should be compact with the stress on the line of the body, arms, head and legs.

FEET

Basic foot position, beats and sequences

In the Andalusian and Flamenco styles of dancing, one of the main features is the exciting rhythm and sound made through the beating of the feet on the floor or stage. These can be varied in many ways and the combination is unlimited, from single beats to extremely complicated variations. Correct footwear should give support to the foot and help to produce good beats. The lady should have a shoe with a fairly wide and strong heel, the base being about 30mm diameter. The height of the heel varies but is usually between 50 and 75mm. The style of shoe has changed over the years with a fashion amongst Spanish dancers for novelty, the shoe sometimes being court, or one-bar straight across, one-bar at an angle, or a lace-up, but not backless. The foot should fit easily but not too tightly into the shoe. A common practice is to have very small nails with a largish head hammered into the heel, so giving a flat surface of metal. Sometimes a metal plate is attached to the heel and also to the toe cap. These are used more by the professional artist. The metal covering does help to produce a stronger sound on stage but it can also ruin a studio or ballroom floor, so care is needed when buying shoes.

Footwear for the man is usually an elastic sided boot with a moderate heel, higher than an ordinary walking shoe and more like a cowboy heel, between 40 and 50mm. The heels can be nailed or plated but this is not recommended.

If ordering shoes from a theatrical shoe shop always ask for a Spanish Dance shoe with a Spanish heel; these are different from the ordinary national or character shoes, which have a lower and broader heel. In Spain it is advisable to find a theatrical shoe maker or shop rather than a local cobbler, allowing plenty of time when ordering.

When performing beats, the knees are relaxed and act as a spring to the body. To beat with straight knees or too much tension will cause a jarring action to the spine. The feet are kept fairly close to each other and well under the body. When travelling either forward or backward, the steps are kept small and neat, and the knees kept fairly close together in order to give a good line. The beats are executed with the feet straight forward or very slightly turned out (if both heels are together then, by the clock, they should read 10 minutes to 2 o'clock!). Make each beat produce a clear sound, and avoid a muffled or scuffed beat like wiping feet on a mat. Listen for a sharp, clear ring.

Foot Positions

There are five positions of the feet and five beaten actions of the foot to study.

Positions

1st   (Fig.1) Stand with heels together, feet pointing straight forward or very slightly apart.

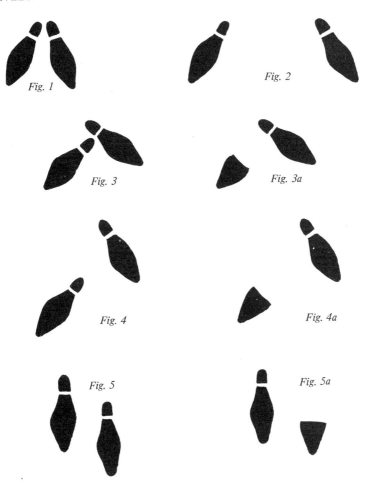

Fig. 1

Fig. 2

Fig. 3

Fig. 3a

Fig. 4

Fig. 4a

Fig. 5

Fig. 5a

2nd (Fig.2) Feet are about 6 or 7 inches apart.

3rd (Fig.3) Right heel against the instep of the left foot or vice versa. Both feet are flat and slightly turned out.

3rd Raised (Fig.3a) As in 3rd, but the heel of the right foot is raised from the ground, the ball of the foot keeps contact with the ground, the right knee bends slightly. This position can also be taken with the weight on the front foot and the heel of the back foot raised.

4th (Fig.4) One foot is placed forward in front of the other, both feet slightly turned out. If standing in a 3rd position right foot in front, step forward with the right foot a distance of about 7 or 8 inches, the right heel should be roughly in line with the instep. This position can also be taken by stepping back.

4th Raised (Fig.4a) As in 4th but the front heel is raised from the ground, the ball of the foot keeps contact with the ground, the knee is bent slightly.

5th (Fig.5) Right foot is crossed over the left foot or vice versa. The position is similar to a 1st position with both feet pointing straight forward. The knees are relaxed slightly.

5th   Raised (Fig.5a) As in 5th but the right heel is raised from the ground, the ball of the foot keeps contact with the ground, the right knee relaxed, the left leg stretched or vice versa.

Foot Actions

1. Stamp with the whole foot

The foot is lifted upwards from the floor and brought down with a sharp stamp.

2. Toe Beat

This beat is executed with the ball of the foot only. The foot is lifted upwards from the floor and the ball of the foot strikes the floor, the heel remaining raised. Avoid a scuff or sliding action of the foot forward. The sound must be clear and sharp. (It is similar to the action of dropping the ball of the foot sharply down on to a cigarette end.)

3. Heel Beat

The ball of the foot is on the floor and the heel is raised. Lower the heel sharply with a clear, strong beat. The ball of the foot remains in place during the beat.

4. Heel Dig

The foot is lifted very slightly upwards from the floor with the ankle flexed and the toes turned up. The heel only strikes the floor with a sharp digging action, the toe remains lifted and does not touch the floor.

5. Toe Tap

The foot is lifted from the floor, in a small 4th as if taking a walking step backwards. The tip of the toe taps the floor sharply and is immediately lifted up again. The knee of the working foot is relaxed and the tap can be taken either in a small 4th or 3rd foot position behind placing the tap crossed at the back of the standing foot.

When performing a series of beats the height of the foot from the floor depends very much on the type of beats and the speed of the music. The beats are not taken with a circular action as if riding a bicycle but should be neat, with a precise upward and downward movement.

The following are exercises for foot beats, together with various beats which occur in the dances. Avoid any bounce action through the body, as if on springs, and keep the line of the head level. The feet and ankles must not be tense or loose but have strength and produce good clear sounds. (Estampio, a famous teacher in Madrid, would make his pupils go up and down his studio, just performing various sequences of beats. After a half hour lesson, the feet would be extremely tired but this type of exercise helped develop great strength of action and rhythm.) The performing of beats in this manner is similar to the playing of scales in music. Care is needed when first practising beats; it is very easy to beat too strongly and do too many. Until the feet become strong, half an hour is long enough. It is very easy to bruise the soles of the feet and this can be most painful. Be careful of where you perform them   if you are a flat dweller, remember the neighbours below! A distraught hotel manager in Seville was once frantic because an American student began practising beats in a hotel bedroom at siesta time. During a Spanish dance course held in a hotel ballroom in Manchester, an irate manager came rushing in as sixty people were beating away; demanding that it should stop as the whole hotel was swaying as in an earthquake! Choice of floor, time and place require careful consideration.

The foot exercises for the development of beats are given in two rhythms, 2/4 and 3/4. It may be helpful to think of them in sounds; if performing in a 2/4 rhythm then you may have 2, 3 or 4 sounds to one bar. The 1.2. will have two sounds, 1. and 2. will have three sounds, 1. and er. will also have three sounds. The count 1. and 2. and/or 1. and er. 2 will have four sounds to one bar.

In a 3/4 rhythm there can be many variations of sounds. If the count is 1.2.3. then three sounds will be made to one bar. 1. and 2.3. will have four sounds. It is possible to have five sounds, then the rhythm will be 1. and er. 2.3.

When practising the beats, it is advisable to listen to the sounds and rhythm rather than work too much in counting.

Basic Foot Exercises in 2/4 time

1. Stamps with the whole foot (2 beats to each stamp)

Feet in 1st position. Stamp the left foot (Count 1.2.). Stamp the right foot (1.2.). Repeat using alternate feet.

2. Stamps with the whole foot (1 beat to each stamp)

Feet in 1st position. Stamp the left foot (Count 1.). Stamp the right foot (2.). Repeat using alternate feet.

3. Stamps with the whole foot (2 stamps with the same foot, 1 beat to each stamp)

Feet in 1st position. Stamp the left foot and immediately lift it from the floor (Count 1.). Stamp the left foot and put the weight on it (2.). Stamp the right foot and immediately lift it from the floor (Count 1.). Stamp the right foot and put the weight on it (2.). Repeat starting left foot.

4. Stamp and Heel Dig

Feet in 1st position. Stamp the left foot (Count 1.). Heel dig with the right foot (Count 2.). Stamp the right foot (1.). Heel dig with left foot (2.). Repeat starting left foot, etcetera. This can also be performed in double time counting 1. and 2. and.

5. Stamp and Heel Beat

Feet in 1st position. Stamp the left foot (Count 1.). Keeping the ball of the right foot on the floor, lift the heel and then lower it with a sharp beat (2.). Stamp the right foot (Count 1.). Heel beat with left foot (2.). Repeat starting left foot. This can also be performed in double time counting 1. and 2. and.

1st combination of beats in 2/4. 16 Bars

4 of No.1 Count. 1.2. 3.4.- 5.6.- 7.8.	4 Bars	
4 of No.2 Count. 1.- 2.- 3.- 4.	2 Bars	
2 of No.3 Count. 5.6- 7.8.	2 Bars	
2 of No.4 Count. 1.2.3.4.- 5.6.7.8.	4 Bars	
2 of No.5 Count. 1.2.3.4.-5.6.7.8.	4 Bars	

This can also be danced with No.4 alternative rhythm of 1.and.2.and.3.and.4. and.5.and.6.and.7.and.8. 4 Bars. Repeat the same counts for No.5.

6. *Toe Beat and Heel Beat*

These beats can travel forward or backward or turning in a small circle to the right or left. When moving forward the Toe Beat is taken just past the other foot. With each Toe Beat the foot moves forward. When moving backwards the Toe Beat is taken in line with the heel or just past the heel of the other foot. When turning, the beats are taken on the spot.

Feet in 1st position. Toe Beat with ball of left foot (Count 1.). Heel Beat with left heel (2.). Repeat with right foot and heel (1.2.). This can also be performed in double time counting 1.and.2.and.

2nd combination of beats in 2/4. 16 Bars

4 of No.6. Start left foot and dance on the spot. (Count 1.2.3.4.-5.6.7.8.) 4 Bars.

4 of No.6. Moving forward. The counts as above. 4 Bars.

4 of No.6. Moving backward. The counts as above. 4 Bars.

3 of No.6. Turning on the spot in a small circle to the left. Count 1.2.-3.4.-5.6. Close the right foot to the left foot with a No.1 stamp (Count 7) and ending in original position having made a complete turn. Hold position (Count 8). 4 Bars. Repeat the sequence beginning with the right foot and turning to the right on the last 4 bars.

This can also be danced at twice the speed taking 8 steps to each 4 bars and counting 1.and.2.and.3. through 8. etc. On the turn, close the foot in 1st position on 8.

3rd combination of beats in 2/4. 8 Bars

3 of No.6 Start left foot and dance on the spot. (Count 1.and -2.and -3.and.)

1 of No.2 Stamp. Right foot. (Count 4.) 2 Bars. Repeat with right foot. 2 Bars.

1 of No.6 Start left foot (Count 1.and.)

1 of No.2 Stamp. with right foot. (Count 2.) 1 Bar. Repeat with right foot (Count 3.and.4.) 1 Bar. Repeat the first steps. (Count 1.and- 2.and.-3.and.-4.) 2 Bars.

Repeat the sequence beginning with the right foot.

7. *Stamp, Heel, Dig, Stamp*

Feet in 1st position. Stamp the left foot (Count 1.). Heel dig with right foot (Count 2.). Stamp the right foot (Count 3.). Repeat using the same feet.

This beat is usually executed in a 3/4 even rhythm but it can also be performed in a 2/4 counting either 1.and.2, or much quicker 1.and.er.2.and.er. It can also be performed by beginning with the right foot.

The beat can be taken in various directions. The following steps are all in a 3/4 time.

Forward, very small step forward on the first stamp (Count.1.) and the Heel Dig and Stamp (2.3.) closes in 1st foot position. On every first count step forward using the same foot.

Backward, very small step backward on the first stamp Count .1. close the other foot in 1st foot position as for the forward movement. On every first count step backward.

Sideways, very small step with the left foot to 2nd foot position (Count .1.). Close the right foot to the left foot with Heel Dig and Stamp (2.3.). Repeat, still travelling to the left. To move to the right begin right foot and small step to 2nd foot position (1.), close left foot to right foot with Heel Dig and Stamp (2.3.).

Alternate Sideways Movement, stamp left foot in 1st foot position (Count .1.). Execute the Heel dig and Stamp with right foot in a very small 2nd foot position (2.3.). Close left foot to right foot with stamp (1.). Repeat Heel Dig and Stamp to very small 2nd (2.3.). Continue in this way travelling sideways to the right. To move to the left, begin right foot in 1st foot position (1.) and Heel Dig and Stamp with left foot to very small 2nd foot position (2.3.). Close right foot to left foot with a Stamp (1.). Continue the step as above.

4th combination of beats in 3/4 time 16 Bars.

3 of No.7. Start left foot and dance on the spot. Count 1.2.3- 1.2.3- 1.2.3. 3 Bars

3 of No.2   Stamps. L.R.L. Count 1.2.3. 1 Bar.

Repeat this sequence beginning with the right foot. 4 Bars.

Repeat again with the left foot and then again with the right foot. 8 Bars.

These steps can now be taken travelling forward, back and to the side.
Travel forward on the first 3 bars and execute the stamps on the spot. 4 Bars.
Travel backward on the next 3 bars and execute the stamps on the spot. 4 Bars.
Travel to the right side using the left foot and the stamps on the spot. 4 Bars.
Travel to the left side using the right foot and the stamps on the spot. 4 Bars.

This sequence can be repeated travelling forward, back and to the side but using the alternate sideways movement.

Breaks

A Break is a series of stamps or a combination of stamps and foot beats, usually performed for only 1 or 2 bars of music. The dancer will perform a Break to finish a musical phrase or step sequence, or as an introduction to a dance, when the Break acts as a warning to the musician that the dancer is ready to start.

The following Breaks should be practised using alternate feet.

1. Simple Break in 2/4 and 3/4 rhythm

3 sharp, quick stamps with the right foot. This can be counted 1.2.3. and hold the 4th beat. Repeat using the left foot. Alternate counting could be in even 3/4 time or - 1 and 2 and hold the 3rd beat.

2. Stamped Break in 2/4. Count.1.and.2.and.3.and.4. 7 sounds

Stamp the left foot (1.). 2 stamps with the right foot (and.2.). 2 stamps with the left foot (and.3.). 2 stamps with the right foot (and.4.). Repeat using the right foot.

3. Break in 3/4. Count.1.and.er.2. Hold.3. 4 sounds

Stamp the left foot (1.). Heel dig with the right heel (and.). Stamp with the right foot (er.). Stamp with the left foot (2.). Hold the 3rd beat. Repeat using the right foot.

In the dance Soleares, the hold on Count 3 is omitted.

4. Break in 3/4. Count .1.and.er.2.3. 5 sounds.

As Break No.3 but on Count 3 Stamp the right foot. Repeat using the right foot.

Both Breaks No.3 and 4 can be performed on 2/4 rhythm. No.3 would be counted

1.and.er.2. and would be 1 bar. No.4 would be counted 1.and.er.2.1. hold for 2. and would take 2 bars.

5. *Break in 3/4. Count.1.and.er.2.3. 5 sounds.*

Toe beat with left foot (1.). Heel beat with left heel (and.). Heel dig with right heel (er.). Stamp with right foot (2.). Stamp with left foot (3.). Repeat using the right foot.

6. *Break in 2/4. Count 1.2.1.and.er.2. 6 sounds.*

Stamp the left foot (1.). Stamp the right foot (2.). Toe beat with left foot (1.). Heel beat with left heel (and.). Heel dig with right heel (er.). Stamp with right foot (2.). Repeat using the right foot.

EXERCISES

for Arms, Head and Hands

When performing the following exercises, stand in either a 1st, 3rd or 3rd raised position. In the (A) sections keep the movements flowing, not too soft but executed with a feeling of resistance. Begin fairly slowly and then increase in speed when more proficient. Move from one position to another taking 4 bars in a steady 3/4, then double the speed, 2 bars for the same movement.

Number 1

(A)   Start with the right arm in 5th position and the left arm in 1st position. The right arm moves out to the 2nd position, continues down passing near the 1st position, up through the 5th Gateway position and back to 5th. Repeat this movement several times then begin the exercise with the left arm raised in 5th position and the right arm in 1st position.

(B)   As the right arm moves out to 2nd position, turn the head slightly to the right. As the arm returns to 5th position, then the head returns forward. Repeat with the left arm and turning the head to the left.

(C)   Add a relaxed hand, or a stretched hand, or a hand rotation.

Number 2

(A)   Start with both arms in 5th position. The right arm moves out to the 2nd position and follows the same movement as in Exercise 1. Repeat with the left arm and continue using alternate arms.

(B)   As the right arm reaches 2nd position and passes down to 1st position, follow the movement with the eyes, lowering the head. When the arm moves from 1st position up to the 5th position, the head will return forward. Repeat with the left arm and turning and moving the head to the left.

(C)   Hand movements as in No.1 (C).

Number 3

(A)   Start with both arms in 5th position. The right arm moves out to the 2nd position, curves across and into 5th Gateway (this is now a 4th position) and back to 5th. Repeat with the left arm and continue using alternate arms.

(B)   Head movement as in No.1 (B).

(C)   Hand movements as in No.1 (C).

Number 4

(A)   Start in 4th position crossed (B) (right arm forward and left arm crossed behind). Pass the right arm through 1st position to join the left hand as in 1st position crossed. Bring the right arm back to original position retracing the same track. Repeat this movement several times then begin the exercise with the left arm forward and the right arm crossed behind.

(B)   As the right arm passes through the 1st position to join the left hand, turn the head to the right. The eyes should look straight: forward over the right shoulder, the head straight and not tilted. As the right arm returns to the original position the head returns forward. Repeat this movement several times, then begin the exercise with the left arm forward and turning the head to the left.

Repeat Exercise No.4 again, but this time drop the line of vision and look over the right shoulder at the floor. The angle of the head will also lower. As the right arm returns to the original position, the head returns forward. Repeat this several times then begin with the left arm forward and turning the head to the left.

(C)   Hand movement as in No.1 (C).

Number 5

(A)   Start in 4th position crossed (B) as for Exercise 4. Pass the right arm through 1st position to join the left hand as in Exercise 4. Leave the right arm crossed behind and the left arm will move through the 1st position to the forward position. Pass the left arm from the forward position through the 1st position to join the right hand and the right hand will move forward. Continue in this manner using alternate arms.

(B)   Turn the head to the right as the right arm moves through 1st position, as the left arm moves forward turn the head to the left. The eyes should now be looking over the left shoulder. Hold this position as the left arm returns to the back and turn the head to the right as the right arm comes forward. Repeat these movements. The exercise can also be performed using a dropped head line as explained in No.4.

(C)   Hand movement as in No.1 (C).

Number 6 (with foot beats added)

This sequence is in 2/4. 16 bars.

(A)   Start in 4th position crossed (B), the right arm forward and left arm crossed behind. Change the position of the arms. Both arms will pass through the 1st position simultaneously from 4th crossed (B) to 4th crossed (B). This will take 4 bars count 1.2.3.4.5.6.7.8. Continue changing the arms on each 4 bars.

(B)   The head is looking over the right shoulder and turns gradually to look over the left shoulder as the arms are changed. Repeat changing from left to right.

(C)   The hands are held as in No.1.(C).

(D)   Add No.2 combination of foot beats in 2/4. Page 24.

Number 7

This sequence is in 2/4. 8 bars.

(A)   Arms in 4th position crossed (B) as for No.6. The arms are held for the counts 1.and.2.and.3. and change on count 4, 2 bars. Hold this position and change on count 4,2 bars. Hold this position and change as in the first 2 bars. The arms are reversed.

(B)   The head as in No.6 and changes as the arm changes.

(C)   The hands are held as in No.1 (C).

(D)   Add No.3 combination of foot beats in 2/4. Page 24.

Number 8

This sequence is in 3/4. 16 bars.

(A)   Arms in 4th position crossed (B) as for No.6. The arms are held for 3 bars count 1.2.3-1.2.3-1.2.3- and then change on the 4th bar 1.2.3. The arms are changed on every 4th bar.

(B)   The head is changed as in No.6 and changes as the arm changes.

(C)   The hands are held as in No.1. (C).

(D)   Add No.4 combination of foot beats in 3/4. Page 25.

TURNS

Turning movements are included in the choreography of many Spanish dances and when performed well they can be very exciting. There are many different types of turn and methods of execution. A turn can be sharp and quick or slow and sustained according to the quality and phrasing of the music or the type of dance being performed. The arms are used passing through various positions or some turns combine the use of the arms with back bends. In theatre dances the turns are often very elaborate in execution incorporating skirt movements, back bends leg and arm movements, or a series of continuous turns. A flexible back is required for the lady in the more flamboyant movements.

When studying the following turns, avoid forcing or straining the movements. The impetus for the turn is made by the action of the arms and through the shoulders and waist. Remember the importance of the posture, then the turn can be performed with control. The ending of a turn is very important, it is easy to allow the body to continue to over-turn and the following position or step will then be in an awkward alignment. Whether the turn is fast or slow, the final movement must be controlled and arrested. Practise the turns slowly to gain control before trying them with a sharp action.

1. Walked Turn

Start in a 1st, 3rd or 3rd raised position, the right foot in front if turning to the right. Three small walking steps are taken, making a complete turn on the spot. The steps are neat, quick, and taken on the ball of the foot. When turning to the right on the right foot, the right shoulder follows the foot action and will give a shoulder lead and strong impetus to the movement. This shoulder action continues through the turn, the body straightening on the last step.

Tanguillio

BARBARA LANDER

© B. Lander 1972

Bulerias

BARBARA LANDER

Soleares

BARBARA LANDER

(No Pedal)

Ped.

The turn can be taken with two forward steps, right, left, and on completion of turn close the right to left in 1st position. When turning to the left, start with left foot. If danced in 2/4 rhythm the three steps can be counted either 1.and.2 (1 bar) or 1.2.1.and on the next beat the foot is placed forward in a 3rd raised position (2 bars).

Arms

Various arm movements can be used, if turning to the right, place the arms in a 4th crossed position with the right arm forward and the left arm at the back, or a 4th position with the right arm bent in front and the left arm raised. It can also be performed with the lady holding her skirt and the man his jacket. If turning to the left the arm positions are reversed.

Twist Turns

This movement is the basis of many Spanish turns and can be taken in four different ways, turning to the right or left.

2. Twist Turn Flat

Start with the feet in a 1st position. Cross the left foot over the right foot into a 5th position; the knees are relaxed slightly to enable the feet to remain flat on the floor. Swivel on both feet to the right, making a whole turn. It is important to use the shoulders well, as described in walked turns, and this will give the impetus to enable the dancer to complete the turn. After the turn has been made the feet will untwist and end in a small 4th foot position, transfer the weight on to the left foot and raise the right foot in a 4th raised position. The left leg can be either straight or the knee slightly bent, and the right knee is relaxed. The final movement should flow out of the turn and be part of it.

The turn can also be made by crossing the right foot over the left foot and turning to the left; the ending position would then be reversed. It is also possible to cross the right foot behind the left foot and swivel turn to the right, ending with the weight on the left foot and the right foot in a 4th raised, or to cross the left foot behind the right foot, turn to the left and end with the weight on the right foot, the left foot in 4th raised.

Arms

In Twist turns the use of arm movements together with the shoulder action can help to make the turn swift and smooth. If crossing the left foot over the right foot and turning to the right, place the arms in 4th crossed position, the left arm forward and right arm at the back. Hold this position for the turn and as the feet are placed into 4th raised position, the left arm is raised and the right arm is bent forward in a 4th arm position. The arms will be reversed if crossing the right foot over the left foot. When the turn is made by crossing the right foot behind the left foot and turning to the right, the same arm positions are used as for the right turn. The arms will be reversed when crossing the left foot behind the right foot and turning left.

Alternative Arm Movements

Various arm positions and movements can be used in turns, the dancer should practise using the following movements and so develop a wider range of arm positions.

(1)   When making a turn to the right, start in a 4th crossed arm position as described, but as the turn is being executed pass the right arm forward and the left

arm back to end in 4th crossed arm position as the feet are in a 4th raised position. (The technique of this arm movement is described in Exercise No.6, page 27.) When turning to the left the arm movement will be reversed.

(2)   The following arm movements can be used whether turning to the right or left. Start with the arm in 5th position; as the foot crosses either in front or behind and the turn commences, the arms are quickly lowered to 1st crossed position. When the turn is completed and the final position is taken, the arms simultaneously will move back into the 5th position.

Head Movement

When performing a turn, always bring the head quickly round to face front. This is particularly important on a quick movement for it will help to maintain the balance and give the turn a sharp line. The body and head should establish the final position as a co-ordinated action, not the body taking a position and then the head moving into place.

3. Twist Turn Raised

This turn is similar in technique and direction to the Twist Turn Flat. It can also be taken in four basic ways, either crossing the foot in front or behind as described in Twist Turn Flat. The action of the body and arm movements follow the same pattern but the slight difference is in the footwork. If turning to the right, cross the left foot over the right foot but, instead of placing it in 5th with both feet flat, place it on the ball of the foot. As the turn is made to the right, both heels will be lifted from the floor and the legs will be stretched. When completing the turn, lower into a 4th raised foot position as described in Twist Turn Flat. This turn can be taken either slowly or executed with speed. The movement is reversed when turning to the left.

Arms

Use the arms as described for Twist Turn Flat and also the Alternative Arm Movements.

4. A Series of Twist Turns

A series of turns can look most effective, especially when danced with speed and smoothness. Sometimes at the end of a series a dancer will hold a pose or drop into a lunge, so giving emphasis to the conclusion of a musical phrase or dance pattern. If turning to the right, the foot work is as for Twist Turn Raised. Start in a 1st, 3rd or 3rd raised foot position, right foot in front. Take a small step with right foot into a 2nd position, cross the left foot over the right foot and turn to the right on the balls of the feet. Lower into a 4th raised foot position, the weight on the left foot and the right heel raised. Step with the right foot into 2nd and repeat the turn. This can be executed several times. The turns should be sharp and continuous and no pause made between turns. It can be taken by holding a position after each turn and this is a good way to practise at first and gradually increase in speed. If turning to the left, the position of the footwork is reversed. These turns are only executed with the right or left feet crossing in front.

Arms

If turning to the right, begin with the arms in 4th crossed position, the right arm forward and the left arm back. The right arm passes to the crossed position back and the left carm moves forward as the step to 2nd position is taken, and the left foot crosses over the right foot. At the end of the turn the arms return to the original starting position with the right arm forward and the left arm back. (The technique of this arm movement is described in Exercise No.6, page 27.) When the turns are taken quickly, care is needed to control the arm movements. The arm movements are reversed when turning to the left.

Head Movement

If turning to the right, the head looks over the right shoulder. As the body begins to turn to the right the head still looks in the line of direction and will be turned looking over the left shoulder. As the turn is completed, the head will come sharply round to and looking over the right shoulder. This action is reversed when turning to the left.

5. 'Broken' Turns

The body has a double side bending action and develops a more broken line than occurs in the Twist Turns.

Start in a 1st, 3rd or 3rd raised foot position, the right foot in front. Take a small step with the right foot into 2nd position and cross the left foot in front of the right foot into a small 4th position, both feet are flat and the knees are relaxed slightly. As the left foot crosses into the small 4th, the body bends sideways from the waist to the left, only slightly and not exaggerated. On this movement the body wlll begin to turn to the right; hold the sideways bend until a half turn has been made and the dancer is facing the back. The body will now bend sideways to the right and the turn will continue, to end facing front, still maintaining the side bend to the right. At the end of the turn the weight will be on the left foot and the right foot will be either in a 3rd or 4th raised foot position, the body will straighten to an upright position. There should be no pause, the sideways bends should flow from the left to the right side easily without any forcing or hard movements. Like all turning movements, this turn can be performed either quickly or slowly. If turning to the left, the movements are reversed. Avoid any pushing action through the stomach or tension in neck.

Arms

Various arm movements can be used in this turn but the one described here helps co-ordination and can look quite effective. Start with the arms in 4th position, the left arm raised and the right arm bent forward. As the left foot crosses in front, the left arm lowers to a bent position forward (Gateway) and the right arm is raised overhead, the 4th position has now been reversed. When the body is facing the back and the sideways bend to the right occurs, the arms change into the original 4th position, left arm raised, right arm bent forward. Hold this position to the end. If turning to the left the arm movements are reversed.

Head Movements

As the left arm is lowered, the head turns and will look over the left shoulder. As the turn is completed, the head will come sharply round to face front and look out over the right shoulder.

Faults in Turns

Avoid any tenseness or strain, especailly in the arms and neck. Try not to force the movement. Avoid over-arching in the back at waist level or pushing the stomach forward. There is often a tendency to raise the shoulders in turning movements and this will break the line of the body and develop an ugly movement. There is no definite rule regarding arm positions in turns, various movements can be used. Avoid the arms being too free and wild, or wrapped around the body. Make a definite ending with control and good balance.

The Music

The music of Spain is extremely varied and often very complex. A wide range of sounds and rhythms can be heard, varying in each region and with the instrument being played. In Seville during Holy Week, trumpets and drums lead the religious processions through the streets. These trumpets differ in tone from those that echo round the bullring. Connected with the bullfight are the bands that play the stirring Paso Dobles, in a sound associated with this sport. The bands or *Coblas* which play for the popular dance, the Sardanas, have a sound found only in Catalonia. In the Northern regions of Asturias and Galicia many forms of pipe and drum are used. One dance from Santander has a very strange sounding accompaniment produced by blowing on a conch shell.

Most popular of all instruments is the guitar, forms of which are found in many regions under different names, varying in shapes and sizes, tone and number of strings.

Spain is a land of sounds and rhythm and this is very clearly shown in the music, whether played on a pipe or by an orchestra; the underlying feature is the sense of rhythm and the pulse of life. The rhythms are often accentuated by foot beats, claps or castanets, or they can produce cross accents and syncopation which gives an exciting sound to the listener. It is these qualities together with the melodies and harmonies that have attracted so many composers, both in and out of Spain, to write in the Spanish style.

The influence of Spanish music and dance has been far reaching; the countries occupied by the Spaniards — Mexico, South America and the Philippines — all have a strong musical and dance link. The Spaniards in turn were greatly influenced by the Arabs, whose music has an eastern quality with unusual intervals, especially noticeable in the music of Andalusia. In this region the guitar reigns supreme, an instrument derived from the Arabs and the East.

In the performance of dances, the guitarist and dancer have a sense of unity, in the same way as a pianist is in sympathy accompanying the singer. The Spaniards have a word *sympatico* - this is something that the dancer and guitarist should possess in order to achieve a really good performance. The guitarist can produce a whole range of sounds, from mellow tones to strong chords and finger taps on the instrument. The note can linger or can be cut short, but it is always clear. When playing for the dancer, he follows each step and mood. The dancer is producing rhythm by foot beats, castanets, hand claps and the dance movement in the body, all being clearly linked with the music. The dancer is aware of the rhythmical pattern and design of the music and relies on the guitarist for support. It is not easy to dance to a guitar but it does develop a sense of rhythm and awareness. A pianist can stress the beat very strongly on the piano keyboard which can be heard over the foot beats and castanets; but when dancing to a guitar, which is a quieter instrument, the dancer has to listen very carefully. The music given for the dances in this book has been arranged for the piano from guitar melodies, but the guitar is used for the recording. Pianists should try to emulate this instrument and bring out the subtleties of light and shade.

Music can be roughly divided into forms in the same way as the dances: Regional, Flamenco and Theatre.

Regional

There is a great wealth and variety found in the music of the fifteen provinces which constitute Spain (including the Canary Isles).

Due to the nature of the country and the difficulty of travel and communication, each region has developed its own special style and characteristics which are quite unlike those of its neighbours. In the same way the costumes and dances differ from region to region within a province.

Instrumental music is used mostly to accompany the dances, but there are also many dances performed to songs. The dancers will stop while a verse is sung and then continue, but the song and dance can be combined. The songs are many, sometimes sad and slow, very often in priase of a special Saint. Some of the melodies of Northern Spain reflect the influence of the Celts in their harmonies, as do the instruments used. Others show the Arab and Sephardic Jewish influence in their haunting and beautiful melodies. There are the simple yet very moving songs with a mystical background whose origins have been forgotten, songs which may have been a legacy from the many pilgrims who travelled across Spain to visit Santiago de Compostella. Not all songs are sad, many are full of life and vigour and the singer may add improvised verses.

The music of the people who live in mountain regions is very different from that of the plains or lowlands. Even the key in which a melody is written has significance. For example, although not regional, the stirring quality of a military march or Paso Doble is in a major key which gives the feeling of excitement.

There are many regional folk dance groups and choirs who visit festivals outside Spain, but most of them perform during the summer months at local fairs, religious festivals or as a tourist attraction.

Flamenco

Flamenco music is the style which dominates the Spanish scene today. Many people tend to confuse the semi-popular and pseudo Flamenco with the true form. The wailing cry of a Flamenco singer and the sound of the guitar can at first sound harsh, especially to those only familiar with the adapted and lighter style of performance. One song and dance can sound and look very much like another but, as the ear becomes accustomed to this style, subtle differences are evident.

The music is based on various cultures with strong influences from Arabic, Hebrew and gypsy rhythms and harmonies. It developed and flourished in the South of Spain, particularly the Andalusian cities of Cadiz, Malaga, Seville and Granada. Within the term Flamenco there are certain divisions or styles, according to the song and dance being performed. The two main categories are the *Cante Jondo* - deep song - and *Cante Chico*   small or light song.

Cante Jondo is the older and more profound form from which the other styles grew. In this group, the singer will usually begin with a long passionate cry or wail, reminiscent of the priest as he calls the Koran from the minarets of the mosques.

The songs are often very sad and emotional, expressing sorrow, death and tragedy. Many of the words are improvised, in the same way as a dancer will improvise and embellish steps or prolong a phrase, if required. The music is usually written in modal form and based on the old ecclesiastic mode known as the Phrygian. There are various scales and keys, which give the music its strange quality, the most popular being the key of E major and A major. It is the stressing of certain notes that provides the rhythmic structure from which a group of songs and dances will stem.

For example, the Soleares, Alegrais and Bulerias are basically the same in rhythm but have differences in tempo and interpretation. The Tanguillio (described in the section on dances) is from a group based on the Tango rhythm. Many Spanish dancers and musicians who have been brought up in the Flamenco surroundings instinctively sense the rhythms and harmonies without knowing the technical background. This insight, rhythm and depth of feeling is what is expressed in performance, a quality which for us is so difficult to capture.

The style of singing Flamenco is extremely difficult, especially in *Cante Jondo*. The singer plays an important part in a performance and one which is considered to be even greater than that of the dancer. It is the singer who sets the mood and theme and inspries the dancer. It can be a very moving experience to watch brilliant exponents performing together.

Cante Chico is a group of songs and dances which grew out of the older style. They are altogether lighter in quality but follow the same structure. The dance Bulerias described in the section of dances comes into this category.

Theatre and Concert Music

Nearly every European country has music which reflects the national characteristics and style. Spain is no exception; there are many short pieces for piano and violin and longer compositions for concertos, ballets and operas. Spanish composers are influenced by the strong gypsy rhythms and harmonies and adapt them into exciting works for concert and theatre, while others use regional melodies based on a particular dance rhythm. Many compositions have stood the test of time and have become masterpieces played in concert halls throughout the world.

The 19th century saw the rise of Spanish Theatre music in the form of the operetta or Zarzuela, of which many are still performed today and are extremely popular. These works are essentially Spanish in theme and music, in the same way as Gilbert and Sullivan is English and Offenbach captured French gaiety. The 19th century was also the time of the development of the classical Spanish dance, a form of dancing based on ballet technique, and music was specially composed for the style. There is a whole range of dances based on Bolero, a rhythm later developed by many composers. The Cachucha, a well-known dance made famous in Europe by Fanny Elssler, was similar in musical pattern to the Bolero. The steps for some were based on regional or Andalusian dances, the dancers discarded the firmer shoe for the ballet slipper and gave the steps a lighter and more classical approach. Similarly, the music was often based on a folk melody but written with a light and sparkling quality to match the movement. The appearance of these dances on the stages of the great opera houses of Euorpe developed an interest in Spain which grew and eventually attracted many composers to write in a Spanish style. Bizet's *Carmen* is an example of a French composer's impression of Spain.

The classical dance was eventually replaced by a return to the Andalusian and gypsy styles and the wearing of a heeled shoe. Flamenco dances when placed in the theatre lose much of their appeal and do not transport successfully. Many dancers not brought up in the true tradition find them difficult, thus a type of theatre dance was evolved which became extremely popular. Much of the music heard in Spain today, on the radio, in films, shows and records, is a semi-popular, semi-flamenco type. This style does not have the depth of true Flamenco but the compositions are based on the rhythmical pattern of flamenco songs and dances.

Teachers and dancers interested in choreography and dance arrangement should always study the music chosen before attempting an arrangement. Music is the basis of all movement and should dictate the quality and style of dance steps. For example, it would be wrong to arrange Jota steps, a regional dance, to music which has a strong classical feeling. In the same way, gypsy steps would not suit regional music. Music is not always easy to acquire in England but can be obtained from the main Spanish centre, Union Musical Espanola, Carera de San Jeronimo, 26, Madrid, Spain. Many famous and lesser-known composers have written musical impressions on regional, classical, Andalusian and Flamenco themes and the study of Flamenco and Spanish music is a vast subject which requires far more than a short chapter in a book.

Castanets

The castanets may look easy to play and to most people mean just the clicking of two bits of wood together but, like any other musical instrument, they do need time and perseverance. Once the basic technique has been mastered, it is the combination of dancing and playing at the same time which presents difficulties.

Castanets bought cheaply in Spain are usually made for the tourist, covered with a design, and have no tone. A good pair of dancer's castanets is very difficult to purchase. It is possible to buy plain but unseasoned wooden ones costing about £1, although these do not last long as the wood splits or chips when used. Castanets used by dancers can cost £10 or more. For practice it is much more satisfactory to buy plastic versions costing about £1 to £2 a pair, according to size, and these are obtainable from most music shops in England. Once proficient, it is then worth trying to obtain a really good pair.

Good castanets are made of a hard wood and vary in size and tone. Some dancers prefer the larger size which can be slightly heavy and more difficult to play, although the tone is often deeper and warmer. Castanets are easily damaged and it is wise to keep them in little woollen bags, easily knitted. The tone will also improve when the wood is warmed, and this is true of instruments such as guitars and violins The fancy coloured cord found on most castanets should be replaced by a firm non-slip cord about 250 to 300mm in length, a cotton cord as used for piping cushions being the best buy as it does not slip. The cord should be threaded through the two identical holes of a pair. If the castanet slips up and down very easily then the cord is too thin and should be replaced by a thicker type. One end of the threaded cord should be longer than the other. Knot the ends of each piece of cord to prevent fraying. Take one of the castanets and tie a slip knot with the two pieces of cord by keeping the shorter length straight and tying an ordinary knot over and around it with the longer length. The shorter length should be able to slip up and down through the knot. Both castanets are tied in this manner. Each pair of castanets differs in tone. One is always slightly deeper, known as the male or bass, worn on the left hand and maintains the strong rhythmical beat. The castanet which is slightly higher in tone is the female or tenor and plays the rolls or ornamentations.

The castanets can be worn in two ways. In the peasant or regional dances they are worn on the middle finger, or the middle and third fingers. The slip knot fits over the fingers and the loop comes just over the first knuckle joint. The castanet sits in the palm of the hand and is struck by the two middle fingers. This can produce a slightly monotonous tone, but when played in a group by several dancers the intensity of the sound can be varied and very interesting rhythms developed. Some regional dances are performed with many multi-coloured ribbons tied to the castanet cord to give a very colourful picture as the dancers begin to move. In Ibiza the castanets are unusually large and all four fingers are used instead of just the middle ones.

In the Flamenco and Andalusian styles, the castanets are worn on the thumb to give more freedom to the fingers and produce a greater variety of sounds and rhythms. This style of playing is described in this chapter. Many Flamenco dances are performed without castanets but with the development and popularity of this form of dance, rightly or wrongly they have been added.

The slip knot is placed on the outside of the thumb first and then the loop is pulled over the thumbnail. The knot is over and past the thumb joint and the loop is between the joint and thumbnail. The thumb is bent slightly and the cord pulled tightly so that half castanets are slightly separated. The wooden shell should sit on the cushion or pad of the thumb (Fig. 6).

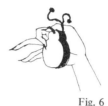

Fig. 6

There are three basic actions in castanet playing; the single beat, striking together and the roll.

The Single Beat

This is produced by the middle and third fingers, the first and fourth fingers are lifted slightly upwards and do not touch the castanets (Fig. 7). Place the middle and third fingers on the castanet, lift them upwards off the castanet and then bring them down sharply to make a strong beat. This movement is repeated continuously and should be practised with both the right and left hands. The castanet must always rest on the cushion or pad of the thumb. Keep the joint flexed and the thumb close to the hand.

Fig. 7

Striking Together

This beat is made by one castanet striking lightly on the one in the other hand. The sound of wood on wood produces a slightly different tone from that made by the fingers hitting the castanets. Care is needed not to crash them together too strongly otherwise the dancer will have a handful of broken bits!

Lift all the fingers off the castanets and with a passing action tap the right hand castanet lightly on the left hand castanet. The right hand moves towards the body and the left hand away. The movement should be small and neat and the tap made by the top of the castanets, not the two edges. This beat could be followed by a single beat on the right hand and a single beat on the left played simultaneously.

The action of striking together is not used a great deal but will mark the beginning of a musical phrase or step sequence. It is also used as an anacrusis or introduction to a rhythm, or to emphasise a quick turn or pass. Some dancers who play the castanets with great skill introduce this sound into rhythmical patterns with great effect. The beat can also be performed with the arms overhead in a 5th position. The right castanet can strike on the left, or vice versa, in a passing action. It can be used in various rhythms, according to the choreography and music, i.e. a striking beat followed by two single beats as described above could be counted (and.1.) or (1.and.), or (1.2.), or (1.3.), or (3.1.). It is advisable, however, to be really fluent with all the castanet beats before introducing this into dances.

The Roll

It is the right hand which executes the Roll beat. (It has been found that left-handed students find that they can roll with more success with the left hand. If this is so, then the position of the castanets has to be reversed, with the male castanet worn on the right hand.) The action is described here for the right hand. The Roll is more difficult than the Single Beat and the following exercises or scales are recommended. When practising beats it is best to place the arms in The Gateway 5th position, avoiding any sharp bend at the elbows.

Exercises for The Roll

1. Using the little finger only, the others lifted slightly out of the way. Four beats on the castanet. Repeat using the next finger only, keeping the little finger raised. Repeat using the middle finger and also with the 1st finger. Each finger should produce four clear beats. (16 counts)

2. Repeat as above but with two beats to each finger. (8 counts)

3. Repeat with one beat to each finger. (4 counts)

4. Repeat with one beat to each finger and then a single beat on the left hand. (5 counts)

5. As in No.1 but make a single beat with the left hand on the first of each sequence of four beats, i.e. as the little finger starts to tap the first beat, the left hand will also execute a single beat. The middle fingers of the left hand should remain on the shell of the castanet and only lift again at the end of the 4th count or tap. The left hand will beat again as the third finger begins the series of four beats. Repeat as described for each finger. (16 counts)

6. As in No.2 but beat the left hand on the first beat of each two. (8 counts)

7. As in No.3 but beat the left hand on each beat. (4 counts)

8. As in No.7 but beat both the left and right hands with a single beat on the 5th count. (5 counts)

Those scales should be practised until the fingers are very flexible and can run easily down the castanet. The fingers should move in a downwards direction, tapping the castanet in nearly the same spot as the little finger which made the first beat. The wrist should not be held too stiffly or the fingers be too tense or spread out. (Very long nails prevent the tips of the fingers striking the wood easily.) The Roll is produced by the action of Exercise No.3 but taken very quickly, smoothly and compactly. The four fingers striking down the castanet should make four clear sounds. There should be no hesitation or stumble. Practise also Exercise No.4, a Roll (and) keeping the 1st finger on the shell of the castanet as the left hand does a single beat on the count of 1. Always keep the two fingers of the left hand on the castanet until they are lifted to perform the next beat.

Sometimes the castanets are too big for the size of the hand, the knot is too loose and the castanets hang limply, the knot can be too tight or the cord too thick. Curve the hand inwards from the wrist, see that the castanet sits well on the thumb pad and, above all, do not strain. Think of them as an instrument, remember that no instrument can be learnt in a day or a week. Playing castanets is unique, as one is playing an instrument and dancing at the same time, whereas a violinist has only to stand or sit still!

Continue practising the Roll and also the following exercises or scales to develop single beats.

Exercises for Single beats and tone

Arms in The Gateway 5th position.

1. Beat both the left and right hand simultaneously on an even count (1). Continue in this manner up to 8. The sound must be sharp and always keep the middle fingers on the castanet once the beat has been executed. The action throughout all these single beats should be 'beat and hold' and not 'beat and fingers out'.

2. Beat the left hand (1). Beat the right hand (2). Continue on an even count.

3. Beat the left hand (1). Beat the right hand (and.). Beat the left hand (2). Beat the right hand (and.). Continue doubling the time.

4. Beat the left hand (1). Beat the right hand (and.). Beat the left hand (er.). Beat the right hand (2). Beat the left hand (and.). Beat the right hand (er.). Continue.

These scales should be practised on various rhythms. 2/4, 3/4 or 4/4. There are many ways to amalgamate beats and rolls for practice. A few basic examples are given.

The castanets should not be played bang, bang, bang throughout, like a pianist playing fortissimo on the piano. Listen to the sound that they make and try to follow the musical pattern and phrasing. Play through the Exercises, starting rather quietly with a light tap and gradually getting louder by increasing the strength in the fingers and the beat, then diminishing to quiet again. In Exercise 2, perform a loud beat on (1) and a quiet beat on (2), continue in this manner.

Castanet Rhythms

Waltz (1 Bar 3/4. Count 1.2.and.3.)

There are many variations in a waltz rhythm, this is the basic or first rhythm.

Single beats simultaneously with both right and left hands (1).

Single beat with left hand (2).

Roll with right hand (and.).

Single beat with left hand (3).

Sevillanas (1 Bar 3/8. Count and.1.and.2.and.3.)

There is an alternative rhythm but the one given here is the most popular.

Roll with the right hand (and.).

Single beat with the left hand (1).

Roll with the right hand (and).

Single beat with the left hand (2).

Single beat with the right hand (and).

Single beat with the left hand (3).

Paso Doble (2 Bars 2/4. Count 1.and.2.)

There are alternative rhythms but this one is very popular.

Single beat with the left hand (1).

Roll with the right hand (and).

Single beat with the left hand (2).

Roll with the right hand (and).

Single beat with the left hand (3).

Single beat with the right hand (and).

Single beat with the left hand (4).

Continuous Roll (Count 1.and.2.and.3.and.etc.)

This sound is used as a continuous trill or vibrato and can be performed on any rhythm or time signature. The sound should be unbroken and flow with no gap or pause between the end of the single beat into the roll, and from the end of the roll into the single beat. It can be used effectively to end a musical or dance phrase, during a slow turn or a series of turns, during a pose or lunge. It is important to listen carefully to the sounds. Some dancers can alter the tone and it sounds like the waves of the sea growing louder and then withdrawing.

Single beat with the left hand (1).

Roll with the right hand (and).

Single beat with left hand (2).

Roll with the right hand (and).

Continue

Once the beats and rhythms are familiar, then perform some of the arm exercises and play, for example, the basic waltz rhythm at the same time. This is also recommended with the Sevillanas rhythm.

Dances

TANGUILLO

The Tanguillo is a development from the much older dance, the Tango. There are three dances which are closely related, the Tango, Tientos and Tanguillo, but each has a slight difference. The Tango, usually written in a major key, has an easy rhythmical quality. The Tientos is very like the Tango in structure but is heavier, rather nostalgic and sad. The Tanguillo is the lightest of the three and more popular. The Tango is thought to have Arabic origins and was popularised and developed in Cadiz, the home of much Flamenco music. This group of dances has a curious rhythm quite unlike the popular ballroom dance of the same name. The music is written in either a 2/2 or a 2/4, the dancer counting 4 to a bar, clapping this rhythm or using foot beats. The guitarist plays the melody with a swinging quality slurring the triplets slightly, which gives a cross between a 6/8 and a 2/4 time signature. Some Tangos, in fact, are written in a 6/8. As in so much Flamenco music, it is the interesting rhythmical structure that gives the dance an unusual and exciting quality.

The ballroom Tango is very different. It is thought to have originated in South America and developed from rhythms brought there by the African slaves, the blending of the rhythms with those of the Spanish Tango eventually taking place. The steps and music became adapted, returning to Europe in a very different form. There is, however, a characteristic style and similarity in some of the steps and those interested in ballroom dancing might like to know the type of solo from which their Tango developed. Steps from the Tanguillo and other Spanish dances could easily be adapted or incorporated into ballroom variations.

The traditional Tango is not often danced now, the Tanguillo and Tientos being more popular. The solo and music given here are shortened and simplified.

Steps required for the dance.

1. *Twist Turn Raised*

    This is described in the chapter on Turns. No.3. Page 38.

2. *Forward and Back Tap step (1 Bar of 2/4. Count 1.2.and.)*

    Start in 1st position. Tap right foot forward in a small 4th position (1). Tap right foot back in a small 4th position (2). Taking the weight on the ball of the right foot, stamp left foot in place (and). Repeat the step using the same foot.

    This step is also danced using the left foot and turning on the spot to the right or left.

3. *Forward and Back Beat step (1 Bar of 2/4. Count 1.and.2.and.)*

    Start in 1st position. Stamp right foot in place (1). Heel Dig forward with left foot in a small 4th position (and). Toe Beat back with left foot in a small 4th position (2). Taking the weight on the ball of left foot, stamp right foot in place (and). Repeat the step but start with the left foot.

4. Ronde Pas de Basque (1 Bar of 2/4. Count 1.and.2.and.)

Start in a 1st position. Stamp right foot behind left foot in a small 4th position (1). Lift left foot and make a small circular or ronde movement, crossing the foot behind the right leg (and). Lower the lifted leg with a Toe beat in a small 4th position, still behind the right leg (2). Taking the weight on the ball of the left foot, stamp right foot in place (and). Repeat the step using the left foot.

5. Swish step (1 Bar of 2/4. Count 1.and.2.and.)

This step travels forward.

Step forward on right foot at the same time twisting the right hip forward (1). Swing the left foot lightly across the instep of the right foot (and). Two steps forward (left,right) straightening hips (2.and.). Repeat stepping forward on the left foot. A quarter or half turn can be made to the right on the two walks left, right, (2.and.), or to the left when the step starts on the left foot.

6. Side Drag step (1 Bar of 2/4. Count 1.and.2.)

This step can travel sideways to the right or left.

Step into a small 2nd position with the right foot, either on the toe or the whole of the foot (1). Lightly drag the left foot across and in front of the right foot with a delayed action, placing the weight on to the whole foot on the last count (and.2.). Repeat this step by using the same foot and continuing to move sideways to the right. The movement is reversed when moving to the left.

7. Toe and Heel Beats (1 Bar of 2/4. Count 1.and.2.and.)

Start in 1st position. Toe beat with right foot in 1st, taking the weight (1). Heel Dig with left foot in 1st without taking the weight (and). Toe beat with left foot in the 1st taking the weight (2). Heel Dig with right foot in 1st (and). Continue these beats using alternate toes and heels.

TANGUILLO A solo dance for a man or girl

Introduction

Start left foot. Enter and walk into the centre of the stage with 8 smooth walks. Arms in 4th crossed position (B or C) right arm forward   Bars 1-4

Step No.1 (Twist Turn Raised) to the right   5-6

2 Stamps in 1st position with left foot and pointing right foot forward to 4th Raised position as the 2nd Stamp is made. Arms as in Bars 1-4   7

Hold this position   8

A. On the spot. Step No.2 twice (Forward and Back Tap step) using the right foot, arms still in 4th crossed   9-10
Step into a small 2nd with right foot and cross left foot over for Step No.1 (Twist Turn Raised) to the right (1 Bar). Hold Position(1 Bar)   11-12
Transfer the weight on to the right foot and repeat as in Bars 9-12 but using the left foot and turning to the left on the turn. Arm positions are reversed   13-16

B. On the spot. Step No.3 (Forward and Back Beat step) using the right foot   17
Repeat Step No.3 twice using the left and right feet   18-19

Stamp the left foot in 1st position (1), Hold position (2)   20
Arms in 4th crossed position (C), right arm forward (or man holding
jacket lapels and girl both hands holding skirt)
Repeat the beats as in Bars 17-20   21-24
Continue the beats as in Bar 17 but using alternate feet for 7 Bars   25-31
Stamp and hold as in Bar 20   32

C. Repeat the step as in A. Bars 9-10 but making a half turn to the right to
face the back   33-34
Step into a small 2nd with right foot and cross left foot over for
Step No.1 (Twist Turn Raised) to the right, making either a half or
one-and-a-half turns to end facing in the front (1 Bar). Hold position
(1 Bar). Arms as in A   35-36
Transfer the weight on to the right foot and repeat as in Bars 33-36 but
turning to the left and using the left foot. Arm positions are reversed   37-40

D. Moving slightly backwards. Step No.4 (Ronde Pas de Basque).
Start right foot. Arms in 4th crossed position (B or C), right arm
forward   41
2 Stamps in 1st position, (left,right). Arms as in Bar 41   42
Repeat as in Bars 41-42 but starting with the left foot. Arms
reversed   43-44
In a small circle to the right, or anti-clockwise.
Step No.5 three times (Swish Step). Arms in 3rd position, right arm
raised and left lowered when right foot is used. Reverse the position
when starting with the left foot   45-47
Step into a small 2nd with left foot and cross the right foot over for
Step No.1 (Twist Turn Raised) to the left   48
Repeat as in Bars 41-44 but starting with the left foot. Arms reversed   49-52
Repeat as in Bars 45-47 but a small circle to the left or clockwise
and starting with the left foot   53-56

C. Moving sideways to the right. Step No.6 twice (Side Drag Step).
Start right foot. Arms in 4th position (A). right arm raised   33-34
Step No.3 twice (Forward and Back Beat Step) using right foot.
Arms as in Section B   35-36
Repeat as in Bars 33-36 but starting with left foot and with arms
reversed   37-40

D. Face the right wall and repeat the steps as in Section D 41-44   41-44
Travelling towards the right wall. Step No.5 (Swish Step). Start
right foot and make a quarter turn on the counts (2.and.) to face the
back.   45
Repeat the Swish Step stepping towards the wall with the left foot
and make a quarter turn to end facing front.   46
Walk freely to centre stage   47-48
Repeat as in Bars 41-48 but facing the left wall and starting with
the left foot   49-56

E. On the spot. Step No.7, three times (Toe and Heel Beats).
Arms as for Section B   57-59
2 Stamps in 1st position, right, left.   60
Repeat Step No.7 twice (Toe and Heel Beats)   61-62

Step on to the right foot and a quick (Twist Turn Raised) to the
right   63
Hold the final position   64

BULERIAS

This dance is one of the quickest and liveliest of all the Gypsy dances. It is
usually performed at the end of an evening's entertainment; the infectious gaiety
and rhythm making an excellent finale. It has changed over the years and some
dancers prolong sections to add certain improvisations, from simple or very
technical steps to comical or sometimes grotesque movements. It is a dance full of
life, in contrast to the sad approach so often found in the flamenco songs and
dances. This type of dance also gives rise to much hand clapping and shouts of
encouragement from the other dancers, which will stimulate the performer to
introduce wild variations. Audiences respond to this type of show, and the more
they applaud the more variations are added. A very accomplished dancer can perhaps
succeed with these tricks but it is advisable for the beginner to keep to the basic
work and not try to emulate the professional.

A Bulerias will often follow a slow sustained dance, such as the Soleares. Many
of the steps found in Soleares are reflected in the Bulerias and both are in a similar
count, although played at a different speed.

Like many of the flamenco dances, there is very little ground pattern and design,
the accent being on the rhythm and execution. The dance should have attack and
clear sounding beats. The beats should be studied slowly at first then the music
should be gradually increased in speed as the beats become more proficient. (A
Bulerias danced slowly would lose much of the character and style associated with
this dance.) It will be found that some of the beats will start on the last beat of a
bar and continue on the first beat of the following bar, the accent being on 3.1.

Owing to the speed of the dance, castanets are seldom used. Alternate arm
positions may be used, the man holding the lapels of his jacket and the girl her
dress. These positions could be incorporated in section B. Bars 13-28, or during
Bars 25-28.

Steps required for the dance

1. Cross Tap Heel Step (2 Bars of 3/8. Count 3.1.2.3.1.)

This step is small and danced practically on the spot.

The step starts on the last beat of the preceding bar.

Start in 1st foot position. Stamp right foot in 1st (3). Repeat stamp(1). Toe beat
with left foot in front of right foot in a well crossed 4th raised foot position (2).
Lower the left heel (3). Stamp right foot in 1st postion (1). Hold this position for
the count of 2. Repeat the step using the left foot and moving slightly leftwards.

Arms
    When using the right foot the left arm is forward in a 4th crossed position
(B or C). The position is reversed when using the left foot.

2. Continuous Cross Tap Heel Step (4 Bars of 3/8. Count 3.1.2.3.1.2.3.1.2.3.1.)

The step is a continuation of Step No.1 but moving sideways to the right or left. Stamp right foot in 1st position (3). Stamp right foot in a small 2nd position (1). The Toe and Heel beat with left foot in a 4th (2.3.) The step can be executed using the left foot. Continue this step sequence for the 2nd and 3rd bars. on the 4th bar stamp right foot in 1st position (1) and hold.

Arms

As in Step No.1

3. Toe and Heel Beats

These are described in the chapter on Footwork and Beats, Exercise No.6. Page 24.

4. Twist Turn Raised

This is described in the chapter on Turns. No.3 and 4. Page 38.

5. Side Point Step (1 Bar of 3/8. Count .1.2.3.).

Stamp right foot in 1st position (1). Point left foot to 2nd position (2). Heel Beat with right heel (3). To repeat the step, close left foot to right foot in 1st with a stamp (1), etc.

Arms

When using the right foot the left arm is forward in a 4th crossed position (B or C). The position is reversed when using the left foot.

6. Stamp and Heel Dig Beats

These are described in the chapter on Footwork and Beats, Exercise No.4. Page 23.

7. Stamp Heel Dig, Stamp Beats

These are described in the chapter on Footwork and Beats, Exercise No.7. Page 24.

8. Cross Back Step (1 Bar of 3/8. Count 1.2.3.)

Stamp right foot in a small 2nd position (1). Toe beat with left foot behind right foot in a crossed 4th position (2). Leave the left foot in this position and stamp right foot in place (3). Repeat by stamping left foot in a small 2nd position (1). Cross right foot behind left foot, etcetera. When the step is danced very quickly the stamps are omitted and each step is taken on the ball of the foot.

Arms

When the left foot crosses behind, the left arm is forward in a 4th crossed position (B or C). The position is reversed when the right foot crosses behind.

9. Forward and Back Tap Step (2 Bars of 3/8. Count 1.2.3.1.2.3.)

Stamp right foot forward, releasing the left heel from the floor (1). Bending the left knee, bring the left foot forward and close to the right calf as if to step into a 4th position (2). Place the left toe into a 4th position with a beat (3). Keep the left heel still lifted, place the weight on to the foot and stamp the right foot into place (1). Tap the ball of the left foot in 1st position (2). Tap the ball of left foot in 4th back (3). Repeat by stepping forward again on the right foot. The step can be danced using the left foot and reversing the movements.

Arms

When stepping forward on the right foot, the left arm comes forward in a 4th crossed position and held forward throughout the step. The position is reversed when using the left foot.

BULERIAS A solo for a man or girl

Introduction

	Bars	
Run into the centre of the stage		1-2
Two stamps in 1st position with left foot pointing, right foot forward to 4th raised position as the 2nd stamp is made. Arms into 4th cross position, right arm forward		3-4
A. Begin on the silent and last beat of Bar 4. Step No.1, (Cross Tap step) using right foot		5-6
Repeat using left foot		7-8
Moving sideways to the right. Step No.2 (continuous Cross Tap Heel Step)		9-12
Moving very slightly backwards Step No.3. (Toe and Heel Beats, using left foot and counting 1.and.2.and.3.and.1.and.2.and.3. On the last count close right foot in 1st with a stamp. Arms remain in 4th crossed. Repeat these 2 bars.		13-16
Repeat Bars 5-12 of A music. Repeat steps as in A but starting with the left foot		5-12
B. Step No.5 (Side Point Step) twice starting right foot		13-14
On the spot, Step No.3 (Toe and Heel Beats using right foot and count 1.and.2.and.3.and.1.and.2.and.3. On the last count close left foot in 1st with a stamp. .Arms remain in 4th crossed		15-16
Repeat Steps as in Bars 13-16		17-20
Two Stamps in 1st position with right foot on counts 1-3 pointing left foot forward to the 4th raised position as the 2nd stamp is made. Arms in 4th crossed position left arm forward		21
Hold this position		22
Repeat stamps and held position but using left foot		23-24
Moving slightly forwards, Step No.6 (Stamp and Heel Dig Beats.) Start right foot, count 1.and.2.and.3.		25
Stamp left foot in 1st position. (1). 1 small step back on to the ball of the right foot (2).		
Close left foot to right foot on balls of the feet (3)		26
Repeat as in Bars 25-26		27-28
In a small circle to the left, Step No.7 four times (Stamp, Heel Dig, Stamp Beats) using left foot. Arms in 4th crossed position left arm forward		29-32

C. Repeat steps as in A bars 5-12 but start with left foot   33-40

D. On the spot, Step No.8. three times (Cross Back Step.) Start right foot.   41-43
Stamp left foot in 1st position (1), Hold (2.3.)   44
Repeat steps as in bars 41-44 but using left foot   45-48
Repeat steps as in bars 25-28   49-52
Repeat steps as in bars 29-32 but start right foot and a small circle
to the right   53-56

E. Moving towards the D.R. corner, Step No.9. four times (Forward and
Back Tap Step.) Start on right foot   57-64
Moving backwards and retracing track. Step No. 3 (Toe and Heel Beats)
Start right foot, count 1.and.2.and.3.and. Arms remain forward   65
Close left foot in 1st position with 2 stamps (1.2.) hold position (3)   66
Repeat beats as in bars 65-66   67-68
Repeat beats twice more   69-72

F. Moving towards the D.L. corner repeat the steps as in first six bars of
57-62   73-78
Three stamps in 1st position with right foot   79
Step No.4 twice quickly (Twist Turns) to the right   80-82
Stamp left foot in 1st position and point right foot forward in 4th
raised position. Hold position, the arms in 4th, right arm forward   83-84

SOLEARES

Solea, or Soleares as it is sometimes called, is a slow dignified dance which requires a great deal of control and style. It is not an easy dance to perform and although this version has been simplified it contains all the basic requirements and movements described in the previous chapters.

The dance is one of the oldest in the flamenco family and was always danced to the guitar and a song accompaniment. It is still performed today with the singer, guitarist and dancer creating an emotional unity between them. The theme of the song is usually that of loneliness and sorrow and the dancer expresses this theme in her portrayal and execution of the movements.

The music has an interesting rhythmic pattern which can easily be recognised. Various beats are accented over a phrase of 4 bars. There are 12 rhythmic beats or sounds which can be stressed. The accenting of these beats vary and several alternative versions are now used. Originally there was a set sequence but the accents have been shifted within the 4 bars. The accents are produced by the guitarist, hand claps and foot beats. In the introduction to the dance given here, the following rhythm is clapped, the first 3 beats in Bar 1, stressing the 3rd beat, the 3rd beat in Bar 2, the 2nd beat in Bar 3, and the 1st beat in Bar 4.

Clapping Rhythm

3/4 1.2.**3**. 1.2.**3**. 1.2.**3**. 1.2.**3**. = 4 bars of music

In counts 1.2.**3**. 4.5.**6**. 7.8.**9**. **10**.11.12. = 12 counts

A recurring phrase with the feet producing the accents is as follows:

3/4 **1**.2.3 1.2.3 **1**.2.3 1.2.3. = 4 Bars of music

In counts **1.2.3** 4.5.6 **7.8.9. 10.**11.12.

In this phrasing the dancer pauses on 4.5.6. and 11.12.

The dance is usually performed by a girl wearing the long frilled dresss ending in a train, a type of costume giving emphasis to the body line and flowing movements. Certain movements have to be incorporated to flick the train out of the way, otherwise the dancer can end up with it wrapped around her feet! It is advisable to use the traditional short dress for practice.

A popular development to the Soleares has been the addition of a quick change of tempo to end the dance. In its original form it ended on a sad note but gradually this changed and a quick Bulerias was added. The dancer will lift up the train of her dress and hold it over her arm, or hook it on to the costume, as she breaks into a quick finale.

Soleares is also a favourite choice for guitarists and is often played as a solo to display technical skill.

Steps required for the dance
Walks

When walks occur, the dancer will take fairly large steps, the knees relaxed slightly and the step made on the ball of the foot through to the heel. The movement is smooth and 'cat-like' with a good arch of the body.

1. Break

This is described in the chapter on Footwork and Beats. Break No.3. Page 25

2. Kick Step and Turn (3 Bars of 3/4. Count 1.2.3.1.2.3.1.2.3.)

This step has an inward 'scooping' action like a reversed developpé.

Step forward with the left foot, the knee relaxed (1). Glide the right foot with a relaxed knee through the 1st position then lift the right knee upwards, the foot should be about 600mm from the ground and directly over a 4th position (2). Circle inwards and lower into a 1st position on to the ball of the foot (3).

Step forward with the right foot and repeat the movement (1.2.3.).

Step forward with the left foot (1). Swivel on the left foot making a half turn to the left, at the same time executing the scooping action. This movement then becomes the action of kicking the train out of the way(2). Place the ball of the right foot into a 4th raised position (3). (This step can be executed using the right foot and turning a half to the right.)

Arms

Hold in 1st position (B) crossed for 2 bars and change to 4th crossed position (B), right arm forward on the turn. (The position is reversed when using the right foot).

3. Toe and Heel Beats

These are described in the chapter on Footwork and Beats. Exercise No.6. Page 2 4.

4. Side Cross Tap Step (2 Bars of 3/4. count 1.and.2.3.1.)

This step moves slightly sideways to the right or left.

Stamp right foot in a small 2nd position (1). Toe beat with the left foot in front of right foot in a well-crossed 4th raised foot position (and.). Lift the left foot a few inches and place the whole foot on the ground, well crossed in front of the right foot (2). Small step in 2nd with right foot (3). Stamp left foot in 1st position (1). Hold this position for counts 2 and 3. Repeat the step using the left foot.

Arms

When using the right foot the left arm is forward in a 4th crossed position (B or C). The position is reversed when using the left foot.

5. Twist Turn Flat

This is described in the chapter on Turns. No.2. Page 37.

The advanced dancer could use the Broken Turn, No.5. Page 39.

6. Cross Back Step with extra Beats (4 Bars of 3/4. Count 1.and.2.and.3. 1.and.2.and.3. 1.and.2.and.3.and.1.hold.2.3.)

Stamp right foot in a small 2nd position (1). Toe beat with left foot behind right foot in a crossed 4th position and taking the weight on to the left foot (and.). Leave the left foot in this position and stamp right foot in place (2). Stamp left foot in 1st position (and.). Stamp right foot in 1st position (3). Repeat using left foot (1.and.2.and.3.). Repeat using right foot (1.and.2.) Stamp left foot in a small 2nd position (and.). Toe beat with right foot behind left foot in a crossed 4th position (3). Leave the right foot in this position and stamp left foot in place (and). Stamp right foot in 1st position (1). Hold this position for 2 counts. Repeat the step using the left foot.

Arms

When using the right foot the left arm is forward in a 4th crossed position (B or C). The position is reversed when using the left foot. Hold the arms without changing when starting on the right foot during the 3rd and 4th bars.

7. Knee Lift Step

This step is performed on the spot and can take 1 count or 2 counts to each movement. The step is similar to Step No.2. Kick Step, and has the same 'scooping' action of the knee and foot.

In 2 counts, start in a 1st position, the weight on the left foot both knees relaxed. Lift the right knee and 'scoop' the foot forward (1). Bring foot back into a 1st position on the ball of the foot (2). This movement is then repeated using the same foot. In1 count, the same leg action is made.

Arms

When using the right foot the arms are in a 4th position (A) the left arm overhead. The position is reversed when using the left foot.

SOLEARES   A solo dance for a girl

Introduction

Stand near the Up Left corner of the stage in a 4th Raised foot position, the right foot forward. The body faces the Down Right corner. The hands are held ready to clap and are near the left shoulder.

Clap the Soleares rhythm, see Page 56.   Bars 1-4
A. Three Stamps in 1st position with the right foot. Arms in 4th
   Crossed position (B) right arm forward   5
   Hold this position   6
   Moving to the centre starting with the left foot, three walks, left,
   right, left. Arms in 1st position crossed (B)   7
   Stamp right foot in 1st position, at the same time pointing left
   foot forward to 4th raised position (1). Hold the position (2.3.).
   Arms in 4th crossed position (B) Left arm forward   8
   Repeat as in Bar 8 but stamp left foot and reverse arm position   9
   Close right foot in a 1st position   10
   The following 4 bar sequence is repeated several times during the
   dance.
   Three stamps in 1st position with the right foot. Arms in 4th
   Crossed position (B) throughout (1.2.3.)   11
   Hold position (4.5.6.)   12
   Two of Step No.3. Breaks (7.and er.8. 9.and.er.10) and hold
   position (11.12.)   13-14

B. From the centre towards the Down Right corner.
   Step No.2. (Kick Step and Turn) start left foot   15-17
   Retracing the track back to finish in the centre, three walks left,
   right, left   18
   From the centre towards the Down Left Corner.
   Repeat as in Bars 15-18 starting with the right foot   19-22
   Face forward and repeat beats as in Bars 11-14   23-26

C. Moving in a small circle to the right, or clockwise Step No.3. (Toe
   and Heel Beats). Start right foot and count 1.and.2.and. 3.On the
   last count stamp right foot in 1st position. Arms in 4th, as above   27
   Repeat Bar 27   28
   Repeat the beats to end back in the centre, 1.and.2.and.3.and.4.
   On the last count stamp left foot in 1st and hold position   29-30
   Repeat C music and repeat steps but moving in a small circle to the
   left, or anti-clockwise, starting left foot and reversing arm position   27-30

D. Moving in a large circle to the right or clockwise
   Step forward on right foot (1). Toe Beat with left foot in 1st position
   (2). Hold position (3). Arms in 4th Crossed position (B or C) left arm
   forward   31
   Repeat stepping forward on left foot, reverse arm positions   32
   Repeat as in Bar 31   33
   Three walks forward, left, right, left. Arms remain in 4th position   34
   Repeat as in bars 31-34 to complete the circle   31-34
   Repeat as in bars 11-14   35-38

E. Step No.4. (Side, Cross Tap Step) Start right foot   39-40
   Step No.5. (Twist Turn Flat) to the right. The turn is slow and takes
   2 bars.   41-42
   Repeat as in Bars 39-42 but starting with left foot   39-42

F. On the spot, Step No.6. (Cross Back Step) with extra beats   43-46
   Repeat this step but start with left foot   43-46
   Repeat beats as in Bars 11-14   47-50

G. The following step is executed in the rhythm of the claps in the
   Introduction.
   Three Stamps with left foot in 1st position (1.2.3.)   51
   Step No.7. (Knee Lift Step) using the right foot, taking 2 counts
   4.5. Stamp left foot in 1st position count (6)   52
   Knee Lift on 1 count (7). Stamp left foot in 1st (8).
   Knee Lift on 1 count (9)   53
   Stamp left foot in 1st (10). Hold position (11.12.)   54
   Arms in 4th position, left arm overhead.
   Repeat as in Bars 51-54 but using right foot and reverse arm positions   55-58
   Repeat beats as in Bars 11-14   59-62

H. Moving in a large circle to the left, or anti-clockwise
   Repeat as in D.31-34 then as in 31-33. Start left foot   63-69
   Step No.5. twice (Twist Turn Flat) to the right   70-71
   Stamp the left foot and right foot forward in a 4th Raised position,
   arms in 4th Crossed position (B).
   Hold this final position   72

Where to see Flamenco Dancing in Spain

Information supplied by The Spanish National Tourist Office.

We list some of the places in Spain where flamenco can be seen:

Madrid
Arco de Cuchilleros, Cuchilleros 17
Corral de la Moreria, Moreria 17, with dancer Lucero Tena
and El Tupe male dancer.
Dinner is also served here.
El Duende, Senores de Luzon 3.
Las Brujas, Norte 15 (with restaurant)
Los Canasteros, Barbieri 10, with singer Manolo Caracol
Torres Bermejas, Mesonero Romanos 15 (with restaurant)
Zambra, Ruiz de Alarcon 7.
Cuevas de Nerja, Avenida de Jose Antonio 43
Villa Rosa, Plaza de Santa Ana 15
Cuevas de Nemesio, Cava Alta 5

Sevilla
La Parrilla del Hotel Cristina, Jardines de Cristina s/n
El Patio Andaluz, Plaza del Duque 4
Los Gallos, Plaza de Santa Cruz 6
La Cochera, Menendez Pelayo 42

Barcelona
Bodega del Toro, Conde de Asalto 103
Los Tarantos, Plaza Real 17
Pueblo Espanol, Parque de Montjuich.

Malaga
El Pimpi, Alcazabilla, also with dance band.
Brasil Club, Pedrizas 76, also with dance band.
Morocco, Casabermeja
Las Terrazas, Pedrizas
Gran Taberna Gitana, Zorrilla

Torremolinos
El Jaleo, Plaza de la Gamba Alegre.
El Madrigal, Urb. Solimar, also with dance band.
El Manana, P.J.Antonio, 16, also with dance band.
El Piyayo, Puerto Rico 2, also with dance band.
Tabu, Montemar, also with dance band.

Marbella
El Boqueron de Plata, Plaza Victoria 5
Platero, Colonia Ansol, also with dance band.
Fiesta, Calle Malaga, also with dance band.
La Pagode, Urbanizacion Casablanca, also with dance band.
El Trianon, Edificio Mediterraneo, also with dance band.

Almeria
Tablao Flamenco, Manolo Manzanilla, Edificio Playa.

Zaragoza
Cancela, Royo, 5
Los Mimbrales, Avenida de la Independencia 19

Granada
Jardines Neptuno, Carretera de Ronda 12
Jardines Alberto, Alhambra (summer only)
Rey Chico Night Club, Paseo de los Tristes
Rio Club, Camino de Pulianas
La Ruta del Sol, Carretera de Motril
Hotel Nevada Palace, Ganivet 5
La Bolera, Ganivet 7
Caves on the Sacro Monte hill where gypsies dance flamenco.

SOME OF SPAIN'S FLAMENCO FESTIVALS

Dates of 'fiestas' in Spain which include flamenco dancing are given below.
It is advisable to check with the local tourist office in Spain when you are
out there as occasionally dates change by a day or so according to
weekends etc. A list of these tourist offices' addresses can be obtained from
the Spanish National Tourist Office, 70 Jermyn Street, London S.W.1.

> Key:
> *The name of the town is given followed by that of its province in
> brackets, the type of dancing predominating, dates and month
> (in Arabic and Roman numerals).*

Arenas (Malaga) Verdiales, Vito and Malaguena competitions. 10-12 VIII.

Colmenar (Malaga) Andalusian singing and dancing competition.
    13-15 VIII.

Malagon (Ciudad Real) Fandango and Jota competitions 14-18 IX.

Sanlucar de Barrameda (Cadiz) Flamenco dancing competition. VIII.

Sevilla (Sevilla) April Spring Fair around 18. IV.

Jerez de la Frontera (Cadiz) 26 IV - 3 V, and mid-September.

Cordoba, May.

Malaga 1-9. VIII

"Festivales de Espana" which include music, dance, operetta etc. travel
all over the country performing in main squares, theatres etc. and top
Spanish artistes take part. Local tourist offices will know if they are
coming to their particular region.

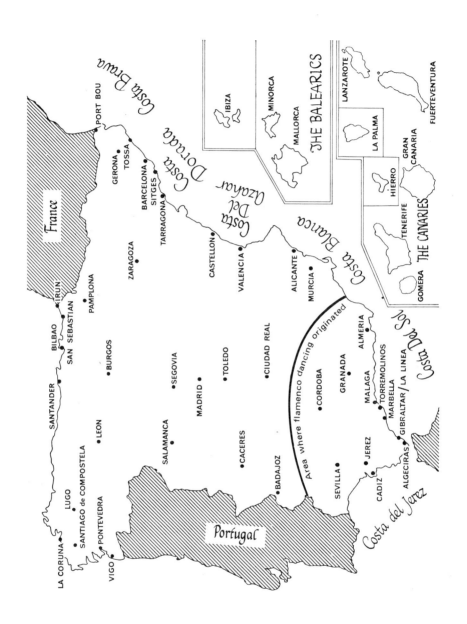